From Mud Huts
to Skyscrapers

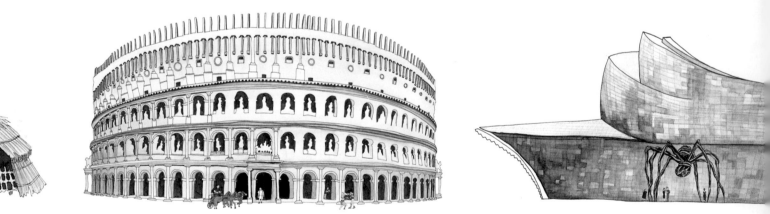

Christine Paxmann | Anne Ibelings

From Mud Huts to Skyscrapers

Architecture for Children

Prestel

Munich · London · New York

Contents

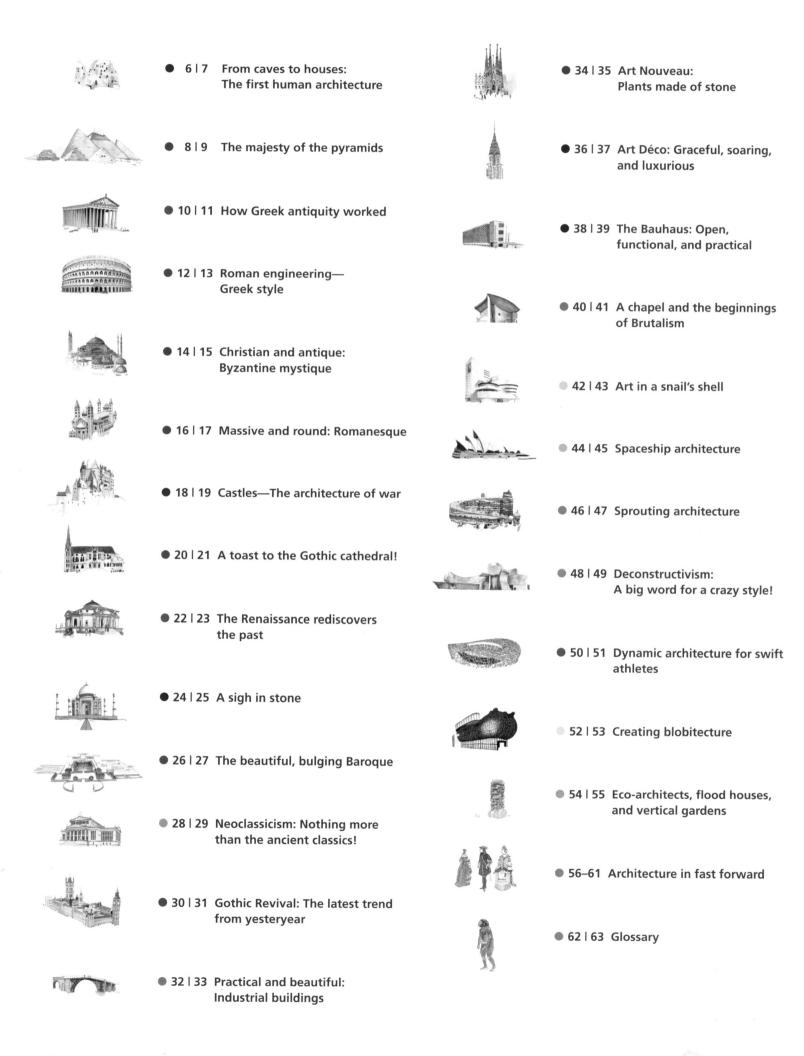

To speak of architectural icons* is to speak of buildings familiar to every child. The Eiffel Tower in Paris, the Chrysler Building in New York, and the Colosseum in Rome are examples of such landmarks. And then there are buildings that not only began a style, but also continued to serve as models for later styles. Ancient Greek temples, for example, have inspired architects in ancient Rome, during the Renaissance, in Historicism, and even in twentieth-century Postmodernism*.

Still other buildings cannot be defined in terms of any one style, but are given their character solely by the architects who built them. Le Corbusier, Friedensreich Hundertwasser, and Frank Lloyd Wright all created architecture uniquely their own.

Even today we admire buildings that have hundreds of years under their belt. These structures have not only become part of architectural history, they have helped people all over the world understand their own cultures. All great buildings, whether they be pyramids, Romanesque and Gothic cathedrals, Ottoman mosques, or ancient mausoleums*, are unforgettable—even if the names of their architects are unknown to us.

Architecture is far more than the construction of buildings. It is the visible chronicle of history.

Christine Paxmann

From caves to houses:
The first human architecture

At the beginning of human history, about two million years ago, our ancestors still ran around on all fours. They sat in trees and were covered with hair. But things began to look very different around 400,000 B.C. Humans lost most of their hair and started walking long distances on two legs—always in search of edible animals and plants. Some of these "hunter-gatherers" lived in caves, while others dwelt in huts made of branches or built into the earth.

Humans relied on such "houses" for thousands of years. But about 10,000 years ago, some people became fed up with their rickety buildings and their hunter-gatherer lifestyle—a lifestyle that forced them to be always on the move. So they created a new way of obtaining food called agriculture. Now they could finally settle down in one place and build towns filled with "solid" houses. At first these homes were only wooden huts plastered with clay or mud, and they were mostly round in form.

Then around 7,000 years ago, people hit upon the idea of using fire to harden the mud. This enabled them to create bricks with sharp edges and corners, and—voila!—the houses became square. Finally, the invention of the wheel in about 4,000 B.C. made it possible for humans to build large houses and even cities: marking the true beginning of architecture.

How people learned to live "indoors"

1 The Terra Amata hut in Nice, France is one of the oldest remains of a hut. French researcher Henry de Lumley tracked down the remains of this 400,000-year-old structure.

2 Around 10,000 B.C., builders decided to press wet mud into the spaces between branches. This technique dried the mud and created a firm wall. Thus the first "solid" houses were built. Unfortunately, all of these homes have long since crumbled into dust, so they weren't really so solid after all!

3 About 7,000 B.C., the first round huts of unfired clay bricks were built; the remains of these buildings still survive in Turkey and the Middle East.

● The Sumerians lived in what is now Iraq, and they were truly cunning people. Around 6,000 years ago they invented the wheel. Finally it was possible to transport building materials over large distances.

4 With the use of fired clay bricks, houses began to be built with right angles. Soon the paths between the houses became streets—and the city was born.

3

The first multi-family homes were rocky cave dwellings.

4

Jericho is considered one of the oldest cities in the world; city walls are believed to have stood there as early as 10,000 B.C.

The majesty of the pyramids

Around 2,500 B.C.—more than 4,500 years ago—the ancient Egyptians did something completely new. They built structures of such immense size that even today we don't know exactly how they did it. The Egyptians lived along the Nile, the world's longest river. The Nile made their land fertile, and it enabled them to create a brilliant culture. Egyptians developed their own written language and mastered mathematics. They also had a unique state religion. Egyptian kings, or *pharaohs*, were considered both rulers *and* gods.

Only one thing was a bit more powerful than the pharaoh, and that was the sun! Sunshine has always been plentiful in Egypt, and the sun became the focal point of Egyptian religion. When a pharaoh died, he wanted his soul to rise as close to the sun as possible. What was more logical than to construct a grave—a pyramid—that reached upward towards this glowing heavenly body? But the pharaoh had to plan for his death far in advance, because the construction of a pyramid could take a very long time!

Even today it is not known how the final block was placed on the top of each pyramid.

Egyptians, pharaohs, and gods

1 *Khufu, Khafre, Menkaure:* These are the names of the three famous pyramids near the city of Giza, and they are all named after the rulers buried in them. The smaller pyramids in the foreground held the rulers' huge "entourage", which included half of the court, the dogs, the cats, and a fair amount of treasure.

2 All the pyramids stand on a square base and are built upwards in steps. The corners are aligned exactly with the four cardinal directions—north, south, east, and west.

3 The stone blocks used to build the pyramids were transported along the Nile by ship. From there, canals were dug so the ships could sail closer to the building site. Once taken off the ships, the blocks were carried the rest of the way on giant sleds. All of this work required tons of manpower!

4 The Khufu pyramid, also called the *Great Pyramid*, is the tallest pyramid in the world. It now stands 455 feet (139 meters) high and consists of an estimated 2.3 million blocks of stone. One block weighs 2.5 tons, or over 2,250 kilograms (5,000 pounds). Just for comparison, an ox weighs roughly 180 kilograms (400 pounds)!

5 In the pyramid's interior there is an ingenious system of tunnels and chambers. It was meant to deter grave robbers and to protect the buried from evil influences. Thanks to this unique method, plus the custom of wrapping up the dead into *mummies**, much information about the ancient Egyptians has come down to us intact.

○ Hundreds of thousands of workers carried out the incredibly difficult construction work using ramps and pulleys. They needed about twenty-five years to complete each pyramid. Their most important measuring tool was the plumb-bob*.

6 The walls of the pyramids were originally clad in white stone plates, which must have shone brightly in the sunlight and been visible from a great distance. Unfortunately, these beautiful plates were later stolen.

The Great Pyramid of Giza is the oldest of the Seven Wonders of the World— and the only one that still survives.

How Greek antiquity worked

The old Greeks loved their mighty structures and their many gods. For them, religion and architecture were closely linked, since many Greek monuments were dedicated to the gods in order to win their favor. The golden age of ancient Greece, around 500–400 BC, was a complicated time. The Greeks often waged wars with their neighbors, but they also created beautiful cities and sophisticated forms of government. The most important Greek city-state, Athens, was named after Athena, the goddess of wisdom. And at the center of Athens was the famous citadel called the Acropolis.

After surviving a terrible siege by the Persians, the Athenians gave thanks to their city's goddess by "bestowing" her with a lavish gift: the Parthenon temple. They built this grand structure from 447–438 BC, on the highest spot of the Acropolis. And the Parthenon's builders came up with a few new things to make the temple truly special.

1 The Parthenon is the largest temple on the Greek mainland: more than 98 feet (30 meters) wide, almost 230 feet (70 meters) long, and over 32 feet (10 meters) high.

2 You can tell by the columns* that the Parthenon was built in the Doric style. Doric columns have a capital,* or top, that looks like a simple rectangular block. But the Parthenon is more than just an ordinary Doric building. For instead of the usual six columns on the façade,* it has eight.

3 The temple's columns are fluted, which means they have shallow grooves running up and down them. They are made of marble, which had to be quarried 10 miles (16 kilometers) from Athens.

4 The Parthenon is erected on a crepidoma, a base with three steps, since the marble temple had to have a good foundation.

5 In the middle of the temple is the cella, or main room. What is unusual here is that the cella's row of columns is two stories high; normally these were only one story high. But what about the Parthenon is normal, after all?

6 The temple's pediments* show scenes of the goddess Athena surrounded by the other gods of Olympus.*

7 Ninety-two small images, called metopes, were carved on the frieze* above the Doric columns. They depict battle scenes that feature centaurs,* Amazons,* and other famous mythological characters.

By Zeus, what a nice shack!

Because of its many columns, the Parthenon was also given a nickname: the "hundred footer."

Athenian leader Pericles ordered the construction of the Parthenon. The famous sculptor Phidias was hired to design the temple's monumental statue of Athena.

Roman engineering—
Greek style

The ancient Romans were legendary conquerors. But because they spent so much effort on the battlefield, they had little time for stylish art and architecture. Then in 86 B.C., the Romans took control of Greece, the cultural center of the ancient world. Now there was no holding back: Greek art and architecture became all the rage. The city of Rome was flooded with sculptures, bits of buildings, and other Greek booty. Roman leaders hoped to make their capitol look something like Athens—full of light-colored stone, stylish columns,* and harmoniously designed façades.*

Emperor Augustus (63 B.C.–A.D 14) helped begin a massive "Greek" beautification of his city. Rome already had plumbing, underfloor heating, and baths. But now comfort was combined with graceful design. The Romans also began to merge Greek columns, capitals,* and sculpture with their own architectural inventions: *concrete*—walls made of concrete on the inside could be clad in stone—and the *semi-circular arch.*

Then in the A.D. 70s, emperor Vespasian (A.D. 9–79) ordered the construction of a building as mighty as Rome itself. It would be the largest amphitheater* in the world, the scene of Rome's most popular sporting event— the bloody battles waged by armed gladiators. In Roman times, this building was often called the *Flavian amphitheater*, after the Flavian dynasty of emperors that Vespasian founded. But today the building is known by another name—the Colosseum!

Romans in the round

The stones of the Colosseum were held together with iron clamps, similar to giant staples.

1 The Colosseum can hold its own against modern-day stadiums. At almost 160 feet (50 meters) in height, 512 feet (156 meters) in width, 615 feet (188 meters) in length, and 1,780 feet (545 meters) in perimeter, the almost 2,000-year-old sports arena could hold around 50,000 spectators. The London Olympic Stadium will be able to hold 80,000 people during the games.

2 Roman spectators streamed into the Colosseum through 80 entrances, and they could exit the building in only 15 minutes by means of stairs and corridors. This system for rapidly emptying large buildings would be known as a *vomitorium*. The term came from a Latin word meaning "to spew forth."

3 Three stories ascend upwards, each with 80 beautiful round arches. These *arcades* were a true Roman invention. On the fourth floor, 240 wooden posts could be used to hoist a giant covering over the arena. Made of canvas or linen, this *velarium* provided cool shade for spectators.

4 The columns* between the arches show the three different orders (types) of Greek columns: Doric, Ionic, and Corinthian. Each of the three floors has a different order.

5 The interior of the arena is about 180 feet (54 meters) wide and 280 feet (86 meters) long. It was originally covered with wooden flooring that could be removed in order to build scenery or to flood the arena for water sports.

6 For the large, weight-bearing parts of the Colosseum, the Romans used travertine stone from the area around Rome. For the building's foundations and decorations, they used a material that was similar to today's concrete—*opus caementitium*.

7 The Colosseum's crumbling appearance is due to 1) earthquakes and 2) the many medieval Romans who used stones from the amphitheater to build other structures.

5

Rome was built upon seven hills, and the Roman Empire existed for almost 1,000 years!

Christian and antique: Byzantine mystique

About A.D. 300, Constantine ruled over the enormous Roman Empire, which had both a western and an eastern realm. Life in the empire was changing. So Constantine decided to move his capitol from Rome to a place in the east called Byzantium. The emperor rebuilt Byzantium into a magnificent city, and of course he renamed it after himself—Constantinople. Today, the city lies in Turkey and is called Istanbul.

Constantine changed the empire in another important way. For hundreds of years, most Roman citizens were pagans who worshipped many gods. But Constantine had become a follower of Christianity, which had only one god. So the emperor decided to make his religion the most important faith in the realm. Christians had only been around for about 300 years, and they had often been persecuted by the Romans. But now Constantine decided to erect a great church in his capital. And even though the church soon burned down, Constantine's successors were determined to construct an even grander building. In 532, during the rule of Emperor Justinian (482–565), the largest basilica* in the world was raised: Hagia Sophia. It took only six years to complete, but its huge dome overshadowed everything else in the city.

1 The architects of Hagia Sophia designed its giant dome so that it could stand on only four supporting pillars. The dome has a diameter of about 108 feet (33 meters) and reaches a height of about 184 feet (56 meters).

2 The entire dome is constructed of brick, which adds a great deal of stability. The dome used to be decorated with golden mosaics, but these were covered over when the church became a mosque.

3 The dome contains forty windows, which may help prevent the formation of cracks in the brick structure.

4 When Hagia Sophia became a mosque, or Muslim* house of God, in 1453, it received its four *minarets*.

5 Fearing that the dome might collapse, supporting *buttresses* were added to the exterior of the basilica.

6 From the outside, Hagia Sophia actually resembles a small city, since through the centuries more and more structures were added around it.

● Originally, the *basilica* was a type of public building in ancient Rome. It had a hall-like interior and housed markets and courts of law. Later, the word "basilica" was used for churches with a high central area and shorter side aisles. Some basilica churches, like Hagia Sophia, were surmounted by a dome.

In late antiquity, around A.D. 600, Hagia Sophia was considered the eighth Wonder of the World!

The wonder of Hagia Sophia

Today, no one knows exactly how Hagia Sophia's builders created such a giant dome with the means they had at the time.

Massive and round: Romanesque

Around A.D. 1000, during the Middle Ages, there arose in Europe the first distinctive type of architecture in more than 500 years. Medieval Europeans had certainly taken their time to invent something new! And in fact, many building techniques did have to be invented or rediscovered. After the fall of the Roman Empire, much ancient knowledge had been lost. No one living in Europe knew how to build wide roofs or great domes over large spaces.

But grand architecture reappeared after the year 1000, when the Romanesque Era began. People rediscovered ways to use the arch, the buttress, and the barrel vault and groin vault* to fortify a building's structure. These advances in engineering led to enormous churches with cloisters, massive walls, double rows of columns,* and large windows. It was now possible to erect an "Imperial Cathedral" in the tiny German village of Speyer.

Many parts of Speyer cathedral are not actually from the Romanesque period. Fires, wars, reconstructions, and additions have made the present-day building a mixture of styles from different periods.

1 Romanesque columns are square at their base*, cubical at their capitals*, and nicely rounded in between.

2 The towers with their spires were built about A.D. 1100. They have arched openings through which the sounds of bells might be heard—except for the fact that bells never hung in the towers!

3 Dwarf galleries*, or rows of open arches, can be found all around the cathedral's exterior. These galleries may have a funny name, but they are beautiful to behold.

Figures and ornaments adorn not only the capitals* of the columns but also the small arches above the portal, or main entrance way.

The portal's arch is carved in layers, which become progressively smaller the farther back they go. These layers make the portal look something like a funnel, giving it a sense of depth and drawing the visitor into the building.

4 At the end of the cathedral's nave (main hallway) is a vaulted, semicircular space called the apse. Here stands the altar, where important rituals of the church service take place. Apses existed in ancient Roman and Byzantine* buildings, and they were adopted by Romanesque architects.

Speyer:
A village gets a cathedral

Many medieval emperors are buried in the cathedral.

Today, Speyer Cathedral is the largest Romanesque church in Europe.

Castles—
The architecture of war

In late antiquity, around A.D. 400, Europe was filled with quarrels and warfare. Many people were forced to gather on hills, where they could keep a close eye on their enemies. When there was no natural hill nearby, a man-made hill called a "motte" was often shoveled together. At first, Europeans built wooden defensive structures on these mottes. But wood burns easily, and the early "forts" wouldn't last long.

By about A.D. 1200, some individuals had become incredibly wealthy as leaders of warfare. They could afford to create large, fortified buildings made of stone. These structures would have to accommodate numerous people, of course, especially soldiers and servants. Houses and tower complexes began to rise upon the old motte, with many solid walls around them. Outside the walls, areas for farming and trade were established. These mighty building complexes came to be known as castles.

Over the centuries, however, life in the castles became more and more undesirable. Europe was growing less warlike, and people began residing in cities. Many of the castles were abandoned and fell into ruins. Others were turned into magnificent prestige buildings* for the wealthy. These "updated" structures were no longer considered castles—they were now palaces.

1 One of the castle's towers was always particularly mighty. In Germany this tower was called the *bergfried*, and it served as a watchtower to observe anyone who might be approaching. In England and France, such towers were used as places of last resort during a siege. They were usually known as *keeps* or *donjons*.

2 Many castles are surrounded by a ditch that helped keep out enemies. These ditches were sometimes filled with water, for very few people at the time could swim. The only way to cross the ditch (or moat) without getting wet was through a *drawbridge*. When the castle was under attack, the drawbridge could be raised up from the inside, preventing the enemy from using it.

○ Cisterns would collect rainwater that ran off the roofs. In the late Middle Ages, wells would replace these structures as the chief source of drinking water.

3 The grandest room in the castle was often called the Great Hall. But people could only use this room in summer. During the winter, it was not possible to heat the Great Hall properly. So the castle's inhabitants retreated to the smaller chambers, which could be kept warm more easily.

4 The area around the castle was its trading center and "grocery store". Servants, farmers, and other people who supplied the needs of the castle often lived there.

5 Wooden shafts can be seen on the exterior walls of many castles. They were originally attached to toilets and used as plumbing pipes—keeping human waste from flowing down the castle walls!

○ Many castles were turned into palaces, while others fell into ruin. Then in the 1800s, the "look" of castle architecture became popular again—and it remains so today.

How the castle was transformed into the palace

Castles remain fascinating and romantic even today. Many are said to be haunted ...

Eltz Castle, near Koblenz, Germany, is a perfect place to learn about life in the Middle Ages. From the towers to the cistern, this castle still looks much as it did hundreds of years ago!

A toast to the
Gothic cathedral!

Did you know that the huge cathedral of Chartres was built in only twenty-six years, from 1194 to 1220? That must have been some kind of record. Chartres' builders had to construct everything by hand—they certainly didn't have any building cranes to help them! And look at the cathedral: It's not only larger than a football field, but also as high as some skyscrapers.

You might ask what made the tiny town of Chartres, France take on such an incredible project. Answer 1: In the Gothic period it was very fashionable to build churches. Answer 2: The inhabitants of Chartres had something that other villages did not have; namely, a gown. But this was not just any gown. It was the gown of the Virgin Mary, the mother of Jesus. And divine clothing could not simply be presented on the kitchen table. People during the Gothic period needed to worship these objects in churches. And they had another goal as well: To build their cathedrals up towards heaven, for that's where they believed God to be!

Everything's in tip-top shape at Chartres!

Eighty cathedrals were built in France alone!

1 Gothic cathedrals often have *rose windows*. These windows were considered to be religious symbols, since twelve spokes radiated outwards from the center—and twelve was a divine number. After all, there are twelve months of the year, twelve apostles of Jesus, twelve signs of the zodiac... Ingenious, isn't it?

2 "How transparent!", the citizens of Chartres would have exclaimed when they first saw their finished cathedral and its 176 tall windows. People during the Gothic period wanted their churches to be airy. They also loved stained glass windows, which not only told the stories of the Bible in pictures, but also bathed the building in rich colors.

● Ornament was the most important thing of all in the Gothic period. Saints, animals, and even grotesque creatures were carved and placed on the cathedral at dizzying heights. When it rained, water would run out of the figures' mouths. This innovation kept not only dampness at bay, but also the devil. The most gruesome of these figures are called *gargoyles*.

3 Cathedrals need many entrance-ways, of course. The grandest entrances are called portals, and they usually feature arches and very thin *compound pillars*.* At the top of the portal is a curved surface that bears the funny name *tympanum*. Saints are typically carved in this place. Such sculptures, called *reliefs,* were intended to help people understand the stories and messages of Christianity.

● Gothic architects made truly high-tech innovations. On the outside of a cathedral, giant *flying buttresses* helped support the building's walls. On the ceiling, *cross ribs* ran down to join the columns,* helping make the ceiling and roof more stable. These supports were necessary in a church penetrated by so many windows!

Ordinary houses are tiny when compared to cathedrals.

The Renaissance rediscovers the past

The word "Renaissance" means rebirth in French. It is also the name of a famous period in history. People who lived during this time, in the fifteenth and sixteenth centuries, were astonished at how many new ideas began to spring up like mushrooms. What had happened? A group of very clever people had rummaged around the libraries of the time and studied the texts of ancient authors, including Roman poets and Greek scholars. They found the ideas of the old writers so stimulating that a new movement called *humanism** arose—in which human beings, rather than God, suddenly stood at the center of everything. Along with humanism came the discovery of single-point perspective,* which made it possible to create images that represented things accurately in space.

Many Renaissance leaders developed a very elegant style of life. Everyone wanted to live like the ancient gods, so they built houses and country estates to look like antique Roman buildings—complete with vineyards, little temples, and magnificent façades.*

One Renaissance architect created homes that perfectly reflected the spirit of his age. His name was Andrea Palladio (1508-1580); and his villa La Rotonda, on a hill outside Vicenza, near Venice, is a true gem of the Renaissance.

1 Renaissance architects loved to use *symmetry**. In their buildings, the right side and the left side of the façade are a mirror image of each other. The square and the circle were the basis of everything in Palladio's art. The architect built all of his houses using these basic forms.

2 Paolo Almerico, an official who worked for the Pope in Rome, commissioned Palladio to build La Rotonda. During the Renaissance, it was very fashionable to build temple-like houses. Even the façade of the house was a sign of its owner's "modern" way of thinking, called humanism.*

3 Entrances like those of La Rotonda are called *porticos*. Each of its four porticos is made up of steps, six columns* in Ionic* style, and a triangular pediment* above.

4 The entablature* above the portico columns runs around the whole villa in the form of a cornice,* connecting the building's various parts.

5 The four little roofs above the columns look like little temples, and the dome in the middle is also meant to resemble an antique building.

Palladio and his villas

Just because your name is Andrea di Pietro della Gondola, it's no guarantee that you will become a famous architect. In fact, this Mr. della Gondola was a sculptor for forty years before his architectural talent was discovered. From that point on he called himself Palladio.

Palladio planned and built more that eighty villas, churches, and public buildings.

A sigh
in stone

Built completely of marble, the Taj Mahal resembles an enchanted palace from Arabian folk tales—possibly something out of *The Thousand and One Nights*. At first glance, in fact, this "palace" appears to have 1,001 towers! But it is actually a mausoleum* with twenty-two domes, four minarets*, and a marble foundation measuring 328 x 328 feet (100 x 100 meters). Construction of the Taj Mahal was ordered by Shah Jahan. He ruled the mighty Mughal Empire, a vast realm that included most of present-day India. The emperor wanted to erect a monument for his favorite wife, who had died in 1631 while giving birth to her fourteenth child. So over the next twenty years in the city of Agra, Jahan's builders created a marble tribute to the emperor's lost love.

Mughal rulers like Jahan had long called upon the best architects to design mosques*, mausoleums, and palaces. Most of these men came from Persia, and they mixed Persian architectural styles with Indian, Afghan, and central Asian ideas. The result was the Mughal style*, which had an almost unsurpassed splendor.

The Taj Mahal: A mausoleum of love

1 There is a strict arrangement to the Taj Mahal, which is named after the emperor's wife, Mumtaz Mahal. The name of the mausoleum means ' the jewel of palaces."

2 The four minarets,* each about 130 feet (40 meters) in height, are tilted slightly outwards so that in case of an earthquake they would not fall upon the central building.

3 The interior of the building is decorated with twenty-eight different kinds of precious stones. Many Hindu* Indians see the Taj Mahal as a symbol of love. So even though it is a Muslim* building, Hindus visit the mausoleum to give their love a special blessing: a true example of friendship between religions.

4 The Mughals loved symmetrical* gardens with watercourses. The Taj Mahal stands next to such a garden, a so-called "char bagh" that has a perfect square shape—980 x 980 feet (300 x 300 meters) in area.

5 Finely chased* stucco and elegant columns,* towers, and domes are all typical of the Mughal style: the more the better.

6 The façade of the Taj Mahal is decorated with arabesques. This is the name for the intertwining plant tendrils found in Islamic art.

7 Today the delicate marble has to be protected from the effects of air pollution. Because cars emit harmful exhaust, they are not allowed any closer than 6,500 feet (2,000 meters) from the Taj Mahal.

....
20,000 workers supposedly helped construct Jahan's marble mausoleum.
....

The beautiful, bulging Baroque

Around 1600, architects in Rome began to design churches and mansions in a new style. Their buildings burst forth with curving domes, grand columns,* and rich decoration—the more magnificent, the better. All around Europe, kings and church leaders fell in love with this fancy architecture. Palaces, seats of governments, and monasteries arose, and the new style was given a new name: the *Baroque*. This word comes from a Portuguese term that means "oddly shaped pearl", but it came to stand for anything that was elaborate and grandiose. Fashion and music also changed with the times. Bulging skirts and grand orchestras provided ideal accompaniment to the splendid new buildings.

One king was particularly serious about the Baroque style: Louis XIV of France. Starting in 1661, he began creating a new palace for himself at the village of Versailles, 12 miles (20 kilometers) outside Paris. The king transformed a small château built by his father, Louis XIII, into a building of unimaginable size. It was actually a royal city. But the center of all this ostentation* was the king himself, who was called the "Sun King".

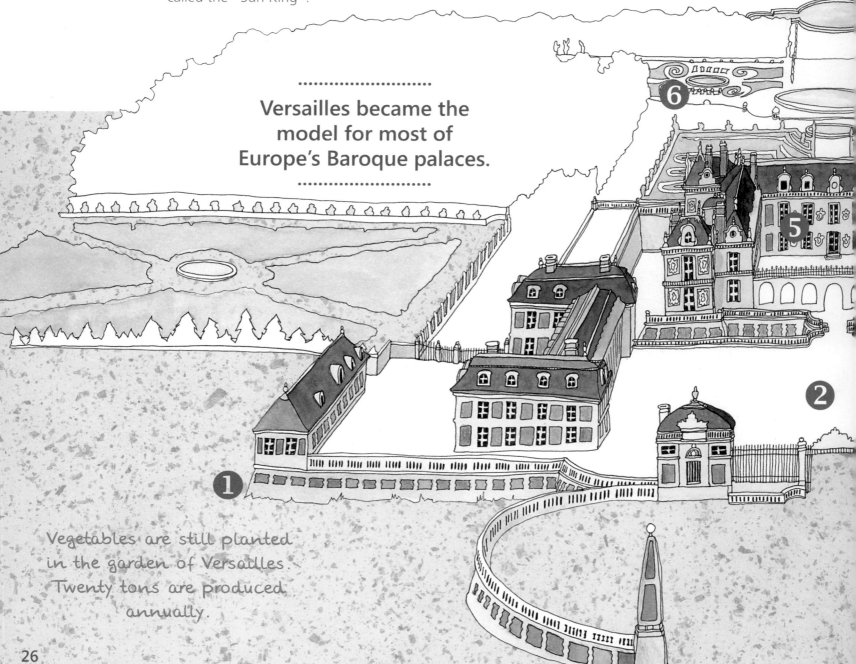

Versailles became the model for most of Europe's Baroque palaces.

Vegetables are still planted in the garden of Versailles. Twenty tons are produced annually.

26

The king as the center of the world

1 At its widest point, the palace of Versailles extends more than 1,650 feet (500 meters).

2 It took a long time to build Versailles, of course. A modest hunting lodge originally stood on the site of the enormous palace.

3 Louis XIII's chateau of Versailles was built in an early baroque style. Its charming brick-and-stone façade* featured large, graceful windows. But the huge palace that was built around this original structure looked much more grandiose, rigid, and cold.

4 In its most glorious period, over a thousand people lived in the palace of Versailles. These included many noble families, as well as craftsmen, lackeys*, and royal attendants.

5 But magnificence is not always the same as coziness: The giant rooms in Versailles were hard to heat and terribly drafty. Versailles' builders didn't even have the technology to install indoor toilets!

6 The Sun King didn't just want a palace of supernatural beauty, he wanted to control nature as well. So he had the largest Baroque garden in Europe designed there.

● The bulging forms that can be seen on Versailles' sculptures, moldings*, and façades are typically Baroque.

7 Plaster and paint decoration gave Versailles' interiors a Baroque look. The walls were covered in sculptures made of stucco*; and the more squiggly they were, the better.

8 There is a striking symmetry* in the design of Versailles. If you look at the palace from its center, you'll see that the left side of the building is an exact mirror image of the right side.

Neoclassicism: Nothing more than the ancient classics!

6

For most of the 1700s, Europeans couldn't get enough of fancy Baroque and Rococo architecture. These extravagant buildings were filled with flowery decoration—plaster shells, leaves, scrollwork, and flourishes. Then, suddenly, everyone found it all quite tiresome! This change of taste didn't happen on its own, of course. New ideas were in the air, and a few clever people were changing the way everyone thought about art.

Around 1770, German scholar Johann Joachim Winckelmann had an inspirational idea. He had traveled to Italy several times, and he had become fascinated with the clear and rational beauty of ancient Roman architecture. Winckelmann wrote a work about these buildings that became a best-seller, unleashing a craze for all things Roman and Greek. Everything that was "antique" was trendy: fashion, images, language, philosophy, and architecture. Soon architects who "re-created" this style could be found all over Europe. One of them was Karl Friedrich Schinkel (1781–1841), who worked for the king of Prussia in what is now part of northern Germany. The name of Schinkel's retro* style: Neoclassicism.

1 Schinkel's *Schauspielhaus*, or city theater, opened on the Gendarmenmarkt in Berlin in 1821. By then, the Prussian star architect had already helped remodel much of that city in Neoclassical style.

2 The theater's portico—the small columned porch attached to the front of the building—looks like a little Greek temple.

● Schinkel based the design of his theater on an ancient precedent: the Thrasyllos Monument in Athens, built in 340 B.C.

3 Columns* and capitals*, strong horizontal and vertical decoration, are important features of the Neoclassical style.

4 When designing the façade, Schinkel used columns attached to the wall. The technical term for these elements is "engaged columns" or "pilasters*".

5 The building's portico has a triangular pediment* on top. It is decorated with bronze sculptures called "reliefs", which depict figures and scenes from ancient Greek stories.

Even fashion was influenced by antique examples, but only for women. Men in the Neoclassical period did not wear togas!

Are we in Rome or Athens?

6 Bronze figures on the staircase and pediments glisten in the sunlight. They provide a lovely contrast with the façade's sandstone surfaces.

7 As at the Parthenon in Athens, the visitor has to climb upwards to get to the building's entrance. Everything in the theater is designed with complete symmetry*: as classical as it gets.

Gothic Revival:
The latest trend from yesteryear

Have you ever wanted to live in a medieval castle? During the nineteenth century, people had a longing for architecture from the past. Life in Europe was changing. Revolutions and wars were overturning traditional European monarchies, and Europe's cities were growing rapidly as the Industrial Revolution spread. All of these changes made people seek security in well-known art styles from the past. In England, the most popular "retro"* style was the Gothic. Medieval Gothic buildings were a familiar sight to the English people. So British architects decided to create a "new" Gothic style called the *Neo-Gothic*, or *Gothic Revival*.

When London's great Parliament building, Westminster Palace, went up in flames in 1834, the path was cleared for a new structure. Most government buildings at the time were designed in French Neoclassical fashion. But French art was unpopular with the English—as England and France had recently fought each other in the Napoleonic Wars. So the new Palace of Westminster would be built in purely "English" neo-Gothic style. British architect Charles Barry was entrusted with the design, and in 1840 ground was broken on one of London's greatest landmarks.

At 13.5 tons, Big Ben is the heaviest bell at the Palace of Westminster.

Living the high life in medieval style

1 The old Westminster Palace was originally built as a royal residence in the A.D. 1000s. Over time, it became the home of Parliament—the law-making part of England's government. The oldest surviving section of the palace is Westminster Hall. Built in 1097, this huge hall was remodeled from 1394 to 1401, when its famous wood-beamed (or hammerbeam) roof was constructed.

2 The rebuilt Palace of Westminster uses Gothic-style supports. These thin, vertical structures make the façade* look as if it had been pulled up by ropes. They are also characteristic of Gothic architecture.

3 The Parliament building's many narrow windows, bays, waterspouts, and towers make it look spiky and compartmentalized.

4 The elongated Palace of Westminster has many towers. The most famous of these towers features a giant clock with the bell "Big Ben", which chimes every quarter hour. Big Ben's chime is often called the "voice of Britain".

5 Limestone was originally used for the construction. This soft stone is easy to carve, making it the perfect material for a building with elaborate sculptures and ornaments. But sandstone is also very susceptible to damage from air pollution.

● People in the nineteenth century loved many aspects of Gothic culture—including knighthood, medieval clothing, and troubadours*.

One important feature of Neo-Gothic architecture is the medieval-style roof, with its fancy crenellations*.

31

Practical and beautiful:
Industrial buildings

①

In 1789, the French Revolution was raging in Paris and threatening the existence of traditional kings and queens. Yet a very different kind of revolution was taking place in England: the beginnings of industrialization*. England had large deposits of coal, and the British were now using their coal to heat the blast furnaces that produced iron and steel. These revolutionary production techniques made it possible to build increasingly large and complex architecture.

The most spectacular "industrial age" buildings were often created for world expositions,* which were held regularly in different countries from 1851. These huge fairs were meant to display the newest innovations in architecture, engineering, and materials science*. They also included dance and musical performances. Nineteenth-century expositions tended to distract people somewhat from the plight of factory workers and miners. Such workers helped make the Industrial Revolution possible, but they often had to toil in miserable conditions.

The Statue of Liberty weighs 204 tons, and her right arm is 42 feet (12.8 meters) long.

Architects of the nineteenth century were artists with iron.

②

③

④

A new world in iron and steel

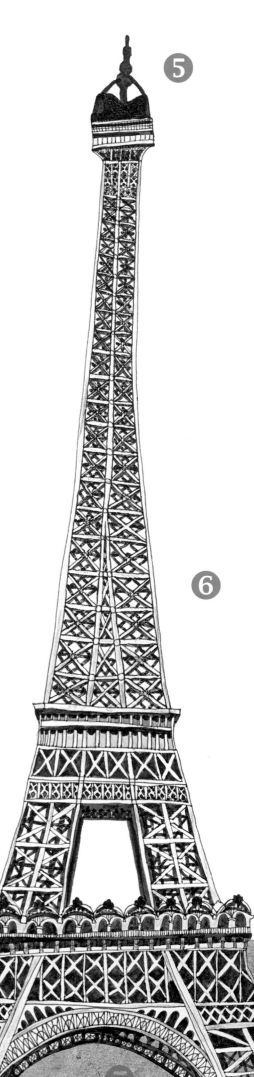

1 To unite the two countries in friendship, the French people sent the Americans the Statue of Liberty, a colossal structure of iron steel and copper.

○ The sculptor Frédéric-Auguste Bartholdi designed the statue. It was constructed in France and shipped in pieces to New York, where it has stood since 1886.

2 The giant iron lady represents Libertas, the Roman goddess of freedom. To help make her stable, Bartholdi enlisted the help of Gustave Eiffel, the builder of the Eiffel Tower in Paris.

3 In 1781, the world's first cast iron arch bridge was opened in central England. The Iron Bridge over the Severn River lies near the town of Coalbrookdale, a birthplace of the Industrial Revolution. The bridge's materials were obtained from a famous iron factory in Coalbrookdale.

4 The bridge is composed of 1,736 individual cast iron pieces. Unfortunately, this construction is not strong enough to support heavy cars or trucks. So since 1934, automobiles have been forbidden to drive across the bridge.

○ The design of the bridge showed that iron structures could be both practical and beautiful.

5 Gustave Eiffel combined a functional* design for a tower with the decorative elements of the industrial age. His unique structure opened the Paris World Exposition of 1889, and even today it remains a city landmark, seen by millions of visitors annually.

6 The Eiffel Tower is composed of 18,038 pre-fabricated iron pieces, which were then riveted—not welded—together on the site.

7 The arch beneath the first platform is purely decorative—but it also gives the tower its unique appearance. Along with the Statue of Liberty, the Eiffel Tower is one of the most famous architectural icons* of the Industrial Revolution.

Art Nouveau:
Plants made of stone

Around 140 years ago, factories and other industrial buildings became common in cities. These huge structures were often built near older houses that looked like temples or castles. To many architects of the day, the fancy houses seemed old-fashioned, while the industrial buildings seemed cold and unfriendly. These architects wanted to give their cities a new look, with buildings that resembled nature. So they created houses with decoration that looked like flowers and vines. And most importantly of all—not one of these structures was exactly the same as the next.

Art Nouveau, Modernisme, Secessionism, Jugendstil, or the Arts and Crafts Movement: Different countries had their own term for the new style. And their artists not only made houses but also subway stations, kiosks, bathrooms, and even everyday objects into forms that looked like they had grown in nature. Yet one man, the Spanish architect Antoni Gaudí (1852-1926), outdid everyone else when he began building the church of the Sagrada Família in Barcelona in 1883.

1 If you squint at it, the Sagrada Família looks as if someone had built a sandcastle with wet sand. A total of eighteen spires were planned—one of which, at 560 feet (170 meters), will be the highest church spire in Europe ...

2 ... because, believe it or not, the Sagrada Família is still not finished. It is supposed to be done in 2026, and each year roughly 22 million Euros are poured into the work!

● Gaudí used special *statics** to make his irregular building safe from collapse. He discovered a form in nature that was composed of straight lines but looked curved. Gaudí also used techniques that medieval architects employed in the construction of Gothic cathedrals.

3 The church's east façade,* with images of the birth of Christ, is finished. The rest of Gaudí's lifework, on which he toiled for forty-three years, looks like a giant construction site filled with cranes (which tend to resemble the spires a bit).

4 The interiors of the cross-shaped church seem like a jungle of stone plants, spiral staircases, and twisted, hollow spaces.

5 Colored light enters the church through—that's right!—colored panes of glass, which gives the building a spiritual feeling.

If the Sagrada Família is
completed on schedule,
it will have taken 143 years
to build!

Gaudí's towering dream

Gaudí died as a result of injuries from a streetcar accident.

Art Déco:
Graceful, soaring, and luxurious

During the early 1900s, new art "movements" were springing up left and right. Cubist painters were "cutting up" everything into pieces; *Futurists* were transforming people and objects into streamlined shapes; *Expressionists* were painting their feelings in crazy, bright colors; and *Art Nouveau* architects were becoming obsessed with curving, plant-like forms.

By the 1920s, people began to mix the best parts of these movements into an artistic style that was luxurious and eye-catching. The new style often used different kinds of materials—including machine-made industrial products—and it featured fine craftsmanship and a touch of extravagance*. Soon this fancy, "decorative" art would acquire a fancy name: *Art Déco*.

Art Déco started in Europe, primarily in Paris and Vienna. But it soon spread to the United States. The American film industry fell in love with the new style, creating hundreds of movies with Art Déco sets. American cities, too, wanted to remake themselves in Art Déco fashion. And nowhere would the new style have a greater impact than in New York City. Art Déco skyscrapers, such as the Chrysler Building of 1930, reshaped New York's skyline.

1 At 1,046 feet (319 meters) high, the Chrysler Building was the tallest structure in the world for exactly one year. The Empire State Building, which was built 1,250 feet (381 meters) high, took its place in 1931.

2 The spire of the Chrysler Building is truly striking: A six-story crown of stainless steel.

3 The Chrysler Building's developers, including architect William van Alen, were competing with the builders of the Bank of Manhattan tower to see who could construct New York City's tallest skyscraper. So van Alen kept the spire of his building concealed until the rest of the structure was finished. When the lightweight spire (with its extendable antenna) was finally put into place, the Chrysler Building had won the competition.

4 The Chrysler Building actually has fenders, hood ornaments, and hubcaps built into it! Walter P. Chrysler wanted his skyscraper to celebrate the automobiles that his company—the Chrysler Corporation—manufactured.

5 The interiors of the high-rise structure are luxurious, and they include eighteen elevators.

6 The building's sash windows are still in their original condition and can be opened—even on the seventy-seventh floor!

● The Chrysler Building was constructed with remarkable speed—from September of 1928 to May of 1930. But during that short period, the United States went from economic prosperity to the Great Depression. New York's building boom would soon come to an end.

7 Florescent lighting illuminates the building at night. This feature helps make the skyscraper a colorful symbol of New York.

> In addition to 29,961 tons of steel, the building contains 3,826,000 bricks and roughly 5,000 windows.

A beautiful style decorates the world

The steel pyramid is known as the vertex, a Latin word for "crown". This structure weighs about 30 tons-remarkably light for something so enomous!

1

2

3

4

5

6

7

The Bauhaus:
Open, functional, and practical

In 1925, architect Walter Gropius designed a new building in Dessau, Germany, for a school of art, architecture, and design. His revolutionary structure was perfectly adapted to its function—that is, it was meant to show on the outside what happened on the inside. This "open" spirit could be seen in the school's huge "walls" of glass, which flooded the building with light and made its inhabitants feel like they were living and working in the midst of nature. Gropius's design would influence many generations of architects, even those living today.

The new school was called the Bauhaus, and its "house" contained workshops, offices, classrooms, and students' apartments. Gropius wanted his building to reflect the new kind of art that Bauhaus instructors would teach. This art would be both practical and beautiful. It would feature modern materials and geometric shapes, and it would avoid frilly decoration. Bauhaus teachers, including the architect Mies van der Rohe and the stage designer Oskar Schlemmer, saw themselves as trailblazers for a new artistic life. They were soon imitated and followed throughout much of Europe—and eventually in the United States and elsewhere. For this reason, the Bauhaus style came to be called the "International Style".

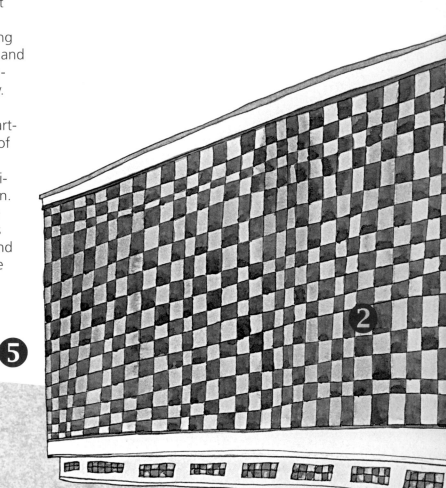

❶ The Bauhaus building seems to be assembled from many different structures, or wings. One wing housed workshops, another housed student apartments, and still another housed classrooms. All of these wings are connected by a "floating" bridge.

❷ Glass plays a crucial role in the Bauhaus. The glass façades* unite the exterior and the interior, making the building seem light and transparent.

❸ In the places where the façade is not made of glass or steel, it is often white. Delicate balconies project outwards. Everything is meant to appear almost weightless.

❹ Gropius designed all the wings of the Bauhaus to be the same height and to have the same flat roof. He wanted to express that all of his school's functions were of equal value.

❺ The glass façade of the workshop wing was partially destroyed in 1945, during the Second World War, and rebuilt again in 1976. It was originally made with a kind of glass that sparkled in the sunlight.

● The Bauhaus closed in 1933 because Germany's National Socialist (Nazi) government rejected modern, artistic architecture.

● Bauhaus artists left nothing to chance and designed everything from scratch, from wastepaper baskets to toothpicks. So it's no surprise that almost all the Bauhaus's furniture and dishes were created especially for the school.

A modern "house"
for a modern art school

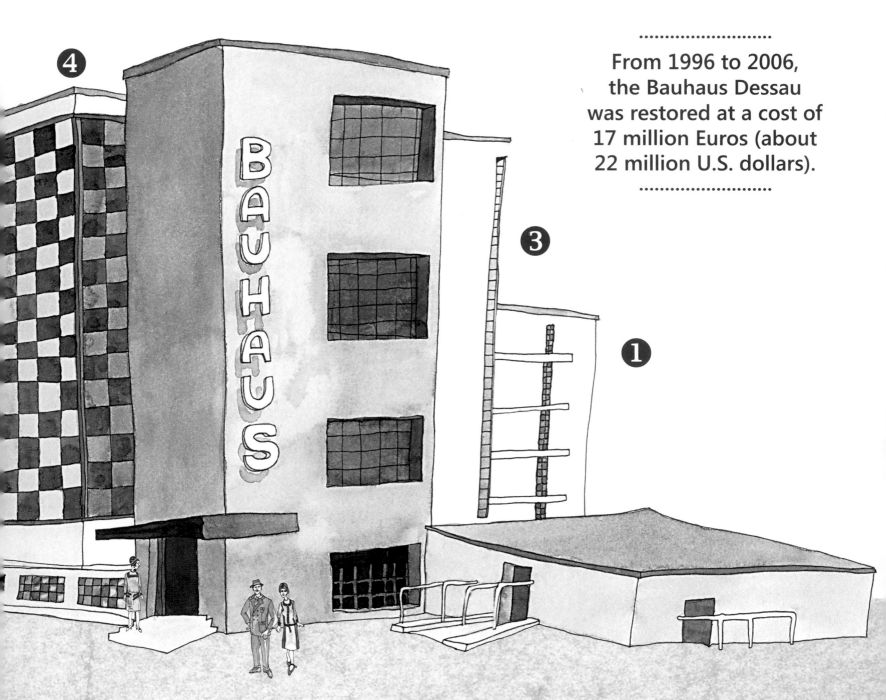

From 1996 to 2006, the Bauhaus Dessau was restored at a cost of 17 million Euros (about 22 million U.S. dollars).

The Bauhaus has been named a UNESCO World Heritage Site.

A chapel and the beginnings of Brutalism

❺

At the foot of the Vosges Mountains in eastern France, a small hill has been considered sacred for centuries. Many churches have been built on the site, which lies above the village of Ronchamp, and Christian pilgrims have long traveled there to worship. In the 1950s, French-Swiss architect Le Corbusier was asked to build a new pilgrimage church on the hill. His building would soon become an architectural icon*.

Notre Dame du Haut de Ronchamp is made of solid exposed concrete (in French, "béton brut", or "raw concrete"). Le Corbusier was fascinated by the material, which was relatively new at the time. To him, concrete represented the future. Corbusier was also a sculptor, painter, city planner, furniture designer, and author. He created buildings that were designed to be works of art in themselves—unadorned, functional*, and completely unique. And the Ronchamp chapel looks like no other church in the world. Thick, curving walls; slit-like windows; a massive, sloping roof; and windowless towers all make the building resemble a defensive fortress. So it's not surprising that Le Corbusier's style is sometimes known as *Brutalist*—a term derived from the concrete material he so admired.

❹

....
In 1929, Le Corbusier designed a chair that is still manufactured today.
....

❶ The chapel's roof is made of two concrete shells, and it sits like a hat upon the walls.

❷ The heavy exterior walls are curved; sometimes they are *concave* (curved inward), other times *convex* (curved outward). The eastern wall is designed as an open-air chapel with an altar, gallery, and chancel. It includes space for 1,200 pilgrims. Only 200 worshippers can fit inside the building.

Ronchamp—Religion in concrete

Le Corbusier designed famous buildings in Europe, India, and other places around the world.

3 The south wall contains more than twenty different colored windows, their shapes varying from thin slits to rectangles. They provide the cave-like interior with beautiful, mysterious light.

4 For the south side of Ronchamp, Le Corbusier also designed a door with colorful enamel plates. Aside from the windows, this is the only colored element in the church.

5 The chapel's rounded towers look a little bit like rolls of dough cut in half.

6 No two parts of the church are alike. Le Corbusier referred to his design as an "irrational* and sculptural style", meant to surprise people over and over again.

Art in a snail's shell

In 1943, the American art collector Solomon R. Guggenheim commissioned architect Frank Lloyd Wright (1867–1959) to build a museum for his many paintings, which until then had been kept in a hotel room! The new museum was to be constructed in the middle of New York City, and the donor wanted it to stand out between all the steel and glass skyscrapers and brick houses. But how to design something so striking in the middle of a loud and hectic city—a city filled with angular, box-like architecture? The answer: Create a building that is completely round, like a thick snail shell.

Mr. Wright was famous for designing houses that harmonized with nature. His work is sometimes called "organic architecture". And even though there is not much nature in New York City, the Guggenheim Museum seems to have "grown" there. It first opened in 1959, and even today it remains one of the most dramatic buildings in the world.

Mr. Wright's early designs for the Guggenheim included a tower. In the 1990s, these designs were used as inspiration for creating the museum's current tower

1 The main part of the museum consists of two basic forms called rotundas*. The large rotunda—where the art is exhibited—stands next to a small rotunda filled with offices and storage space. The small tower was added later.

2 The exterior of the Guggenheim Museum is kept a brilliant white. On the inside, light cascades down the entire building through a glass roof.

3 Inside, the visitor walks up several stories upon a slowly ascending ramp, which is also the exhibition space. Walking up the museum, you feel as if you're exploring a "mountain" of art.

4 Rooms occasionally branch off from the spiral-shaped exhibition ramp. For the interior of his museum, Mr. Wright had in mind a shape that resembles the inside of a lemon.

Artists used to complain that Wright's museum building was too showy, taking all the attention away from their works. Today it is a great honor to be shown in the hallowed Guggenheim.

Frank Lloyd Wright invented a new American style of architecture. All of his buildings were designed to have a central area where people would gather. In Wright's houses, this area was often next to a fireplace.

Inconspicuously conspicuous

Frank Lloyd Wright made
700 sketches before
Mr. Guggenheim finally
gave his approval.

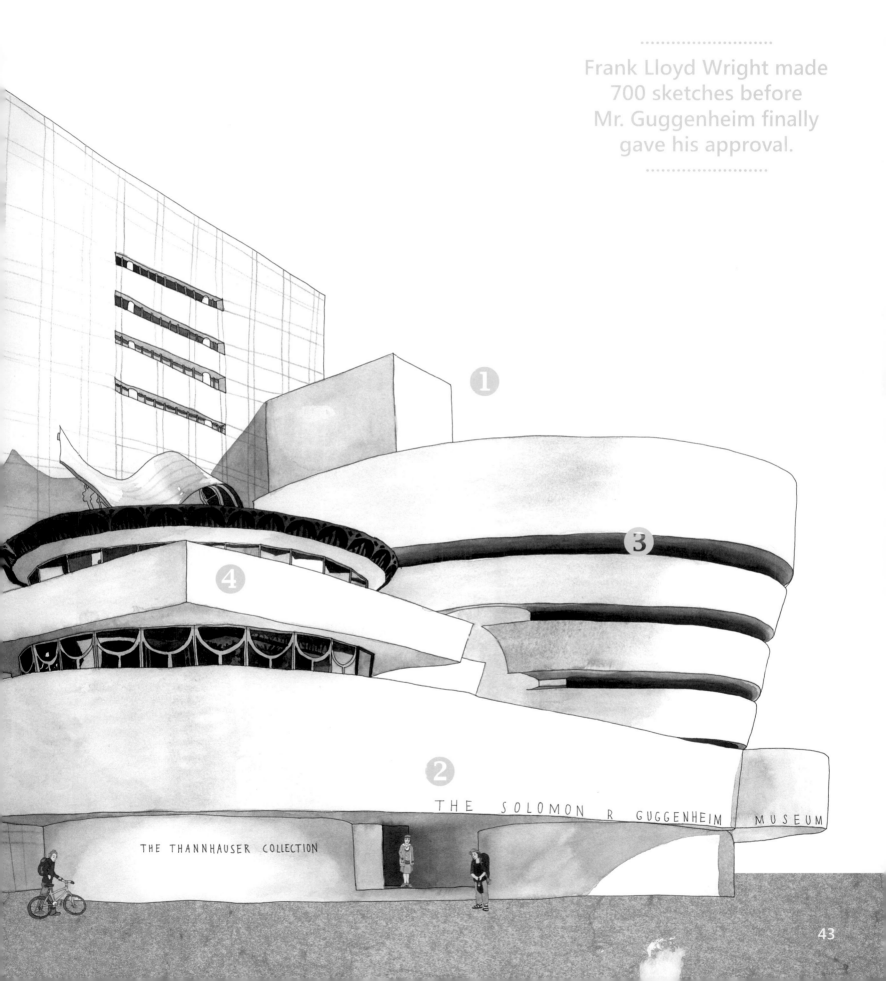

THE SOLOMON R GUGGENHEIM MUSEUM

THE THANNHAUSER COLLECTION

Spaceship architecture

During the 1960s, angular, box-like homes were built all over the world. They were designed to be perfectly useful, and they could be constructed quickly and easily. But few people really liked them. Many found the homes ugly because they were made of concrete, the favorite "useful" material of the modern age. And when they were built in the form of high-rise apartments, all the floors looked exactly the same!

But whenever there is a dominant way of doing things, there is also a counter movement of people who want something different. Many architects wanted to build in a futuristic* way without corners and edges. They also wanted to tell unique stories with their buildings. These architects refused to design the standard "building-block architecture", and they were often called utopians* and crackpots, visionaries* and dreamers. Fortunately, however, some of them were given large commissions in which their ideas could be realized.

The Danish architect Jørn Utzon (1918–2008) was one of them. His design for the Sydney Opera House made him and the city of Sidney, Australia famous; even though his clients got cold feet during the construction process because everything took too long and became too expensive. As a matter of fact, the process wound up being two times longer and fifteen times costlier than planned! But no one thinks about these problems anymore, and today the building is a UNESCO World Heritage Site.

In 2003 Utzon was rightfully awarded the Pritzker Prize, the "Oscar" for architects.

Australia's monarch, Queen Elizabeth II, christened the building in 1973. Jørn Utzon was not invited to the ceremony!

Australia's funky landmark

1 On its peninsula in the harbor, the silhouette of the Sydney Opera House appears from a distance like a sailboat; up close it looks like carefully peeled sections of an orange.

2 Was Utzon thinking of his childhood when he drew up the designs? Jørn came from a family of yacht builders. Each of the roof sails, which look as if they're filled with wind, is covered with white Swedish tiles. The magnificent roof soars up 220 feet (67 meters) into the air.

3 After visiting a design show in Stockholm, Sweden in 1930, Utzon's family banished everything dark from their home in favor of light colors and illumination. Is it any wonder that Utzon created such a bright, airy work?

4 Construction on the building began in 1959. But the curves of the elaborate roof structure had to be recalculated several times. There were no computers at the time that could do this work, so the building wasn't finished until 1973!

◉ As the construction process became more and more expensive, the relationship between Utzon and his clients grew worse. Utzon finally resigned from the project in 1966, and a team of architects completed the building.

5 To cut costs, the new architects rejected many of Utzon's plans for the building's interior decoration. Today, these interiors do not really match the fascinating outer shell. But the building complex still attracts a great many visitors, offering them not only an opera house but also a concert hall and several theaters.

Sprouting architecture

In the 1970s and 80s, people became more and more worried about the environment. They feared that nature was being ruined by pollution and other human problems. Many joined the "environmental movement" to try and protect the natural world. Others simply wanted a lot more nature around them, even in their living spaces.

One artist was perfectly in tune with environmentalism: the Austrian architect Friedensreich Hundertwasser. He called his world-famous building style "vegetative", which means that his structures seem to "grow" like living plants. Hundertwasser was more than fifty years old when his house designs were first built, but he had already been thinking and writing about architecture for many years. From the beginning, these houses seemed as crooked and irregular as if someone had formed them out of modeling clay and then painted them with a profusion of bright colors. The architect's "wild", twisting structures not only resembled plants, they also incorporated real plants on their balconies and roofs. Hundertwasser especially loved the spiral; and with his last building project, the *Forest Spiral* in Darmstadt, Germany, he created a monument to this snake-like form.

....

No two of the building's more than 1,000 windows are the same.

....

❶ The Forest Spiral is curved in a U-shape, which meanders up to the highest point on the twelfth story.

❷ Golden onion domes on the ends of the building complex are reminiscent of churches in Russia or Bavaria.

❸ For the roof of Forest Spiral, Hundertwasser thought up a platform with trees growing on it—trees that could be watered by natural rain.

❹ Typical Hundertwasser: Ceramic beading covers the façades* so that the building resembles a cake made by a sloppy baker.

❺ Trees also grow from many of the windows and niches; Hundertwasser called them "tree tenants".

Hundertwasser used recycled* cement to build this playful and environmentally-friendly apartment building.

❻ The bands of earth tones that wrap around the structure are meant to symbolize layers of the earth, as if the apartment was growing.

❼ Hundertwasser built without right angles because such forms rarely occur in nature.

Hundertwasser's Hill Houses

Hundertwasser died suddenly in the year 2000, two months before Forest Spiral was completed. He was travelling from New Zealand to Europe on board an ocean liner.

Deconstructivism:
A big word for a crazy style!

Most anyone can build architecture with straight lines and right angles. Ruler, protractor, compass—and there's your house! During the 1980s, it was all the rage to make buildings with classical-style columns* and square windows: everything very orderly. But in the following decade, a small group of architects decided to try something different. They created a complex new style with an equally complex name: Deconstructivism.

One of these artists would achieve great success: the Canadian architect Frank O. Gehry (b. 1928). As a child, Gehry was always playing with cans, pipes, and other scraps from his grandfather's hardware store. Later, after studying architecture in school, he built fairly "normal" houses with straight edges and geometric corners. But as Frank grew older, he started using computers to help him design his buildings. Soon his architecture became more and more unusual. Gehry's most famous creation, the Guggenheim Museum in Bilbao, Spain (1993-1997), may also be his strangest. It looks like an assemblage of giant tin cans and steel boxes that have been dented here and there—almost like the hardware store objects from Gehry's childhood. Everything seems accidental; but in reality, it is all completely intentional.

....

This extremely complex museum was built in only four years, from 1993 to 1997.

....

Orderly disorder in Bilbao

1 Frank Gehry's building style is only possible with computer programs, which calculate how to make the corners and bends strong and stable.

2 When looking at "Deconstructivist" architecture, people often cannot tell which walls support the weight of the structure. Such buildings seem to be broken apart into forms that bulge forward and recede into nowhere.

3 The individual components of the museum look like broken, rocky crags above Bilbao's Nervión River. Water is reflected in the shiny façade, which consists largely of a metal called titanium-zinc.

4 Frank Gehry used glass, stone, steel, and water for the Guggenheim's construction: building materials that come from the Bilbao region.

5 In the evening sun, the smooth surface of the curved façade shimmers like gold. The fractured surfaces reflect everything a thousand times over, as in a cabinet of mirrors.

● Deconstructivist architects often want their buildings to look mysterious.

● The museum's "broken-up" appearance may lead some viewers to think that a mistake was made in its design. But the opposite is true: Deconstructivism is only possible through the most precise calculations. Otherwise the crooked parts would collapse like a house of cards.

● The Bilbao Guggenheim measures 260,000 square feet (24,000 square meters)!

The forms of the Guggenheim Museum Bilbao symbolize the forces of nature.

Dynamic architecture
for swift athletes

People in China often think in symbols. Even their language is written in symbolic characters. For more than 3,000 years, Chinese characters have stood for animals, plants, numbers, everyday objects, and even human traits and concepts—such as fate, fortune, and misfortune.

In 2002, it was the good fortune of Swiss architects Jacques Herzog and Pierre de Meuron to win a competition for designing Beijing's Olympic Stadium. That stadium, now known as the "Bird's Nest", would be the scene of China's spectacular 2008 Olympic Games. But Herzog and de Meuron did not leave everything to chance during the design process. They worked with Chinese architects who were well versed in China's favorite symbols. These artists knew that birds' nests were very popular in their country. So they helped Herzog and de Meuron create a building that actually resembled a bird's nest—with a 50,000-ton "shell" of steel beams, all interlaced like massive twigs and branches.

4

Nowhere in the stadium do steel and concrete come into contact with each other.

2

The world's largest bird's nest

1 To put it simply, the form of the Bird's Nest is a concrete bowl—which is surrounded by a shell of curved steel beams.

2 The entire "net" of steel is welded together, with each individual piece carefully designed so that the structure does not collapse. The building does not contain a single nail or screw.

3 The Bird's Nest is 1,080 feet (330 meters) long and 720 feet (220 meters) wide. During the 2008 Olympics, it accommodated 91,000 spectators. How many birds do you think it could hold?

O The stadium was opened for the Summer Games of the XXIX Olympiad on August 8, 2008, at 8:08 P.M. Can you guess what the Chinese people's favorite number is?

4 The stadium was actually supposed to have a roof, but this plan was abandoned for reasons of cost. Today no one misses the roof at all.

O Modern technology and computer design is necessary to make heavy steel beams look like they had been bent by hand!

....

The Bird's Nest cost roughly 325 million euros, or $423 U.S. dollars.

....

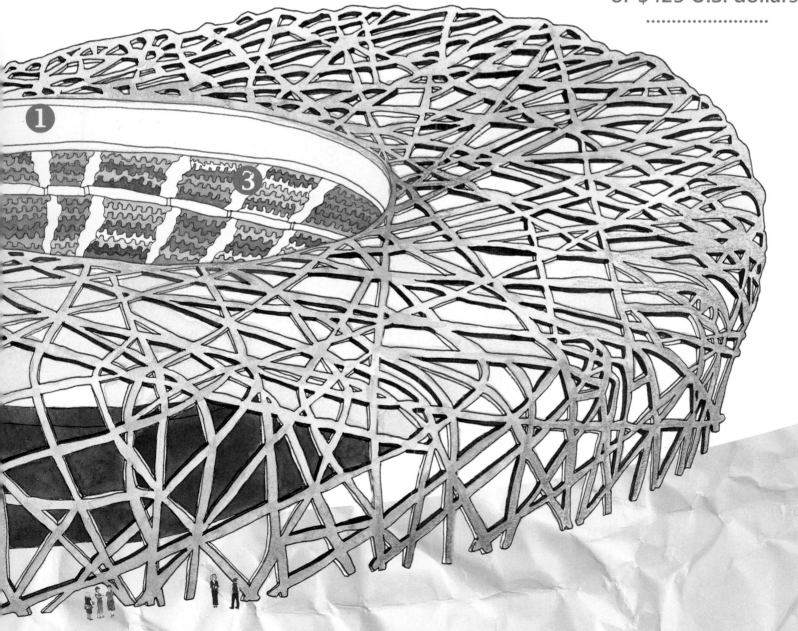

Have you ever seen a work of *blobitecture*? If you have, you probably remember it well! Blobitecture (or blob architecture) looks just like it sounds—a fantastically rounded building that can resemble soap bubbles or squishy slugs. And it always stands out from the architecture that surrounds it. Blobitecture owes its existence to the computer, and specifically a computer program called CAD, or "computer aided design". Using CAD, architects can plan all kinds of fanciful creations—including museums without a single angle or straight wall, and houses in which no two rooms look alike.

Blob architecture was also inspired by buildings that were designed before the invention of CAD. Munich's Olympic stadium was built in 1972, and its blob-like roof is anything but flat! Later architects would use CAD to make entire structures that resembled this futuristic* roof. Two such artists are the British architects Peter Cook and Colin Fournier. They were hired by the city of Graz, Austria to build a new art museum. The Kunsthaus Graz was completed in 2003, and it's a perfect example of blobitecture. Its bulging walls and flickering lights make the building seem to change all the time, just like the changing art exhibits it houses inside.

of hundreds of
e of which are
e next. Yet they
g the building look
n it!

3 At the touch of a button, lights in the façade* can be turned on and off, dimmed, or made to change color. In this way the house itself becomes a constantly changing work of art.

lculates how all
ether, so that there

● Nothing about a blob building is ready-made. Every component must be specifically produced, which of course is very expensive.

e Kunsthaus Graz
hed sea cucum-
ne building looks
" enough to be

● Many blob buildings would fit perfectly in a science fiction film!

term CAD, "Blob" is an abbreviation.
stands for "binary large objects",
fers to the shapes that blob architects
use to create their buildings.

Buildings as bulbous as doughnuts

More than 900 small
lights illuminate the
900-square-meter façade!

Eco-architects, flood houses, and vertical gardens

Anyone who designs buildings today has to think about the future. Space in the cities is becoming increasingly expensive, and more and more regions are threatened with natural catastrophes caused by climate change. For these reasons, a number of architects have resolved to build *with* nature rather than against it. Their whole approach is called eco-architecture, or green architecture, and it's all the rage.

Eco-architects feature environmentally friendly materials in their buildings. They also use computers to design and engineer structures that fit perfectly in their "natural habitat". Such buildings are often earthquake-proof, planted with greenery, and made to use very little energy. Some of the most striking green designs are houses and apartment buildings, which often seem to "become one" with their environment.

1 Dutch architect Koen Olthuis specializes in designing houses on water. He uses water power, wind, and new materials to build homes that are ideally equipped for the future.

2 A specific mixture of concrete and Styrofoam makes it possible for Koen's houses to accommodate changes in water levels. If the water rises due to climate change, houses constructed like this are able to withstand flooding!

3 Around 10,000 years ago, people were building round huts of mud or clay. Modern architects who design houses for earthquake-prone regions have discovered just how practical these buildings were. So they are designing their own domed structures called "monolithic domes". Such houses are cast in a single piece of concrete, and they are especially resistant to tornados and earthquakes.

4 Some monolithic domes have already been built in Florida and Turkey. They look like cozy igloos!

Who would have thought that architecture could one day return to its origins: caves, treehouses, and pile dwellings?

1

2

A mere 237 square feet (22 square meters) of planted wall surface can conserve 1 ton of carbon dioxide each year!

Oases of the future

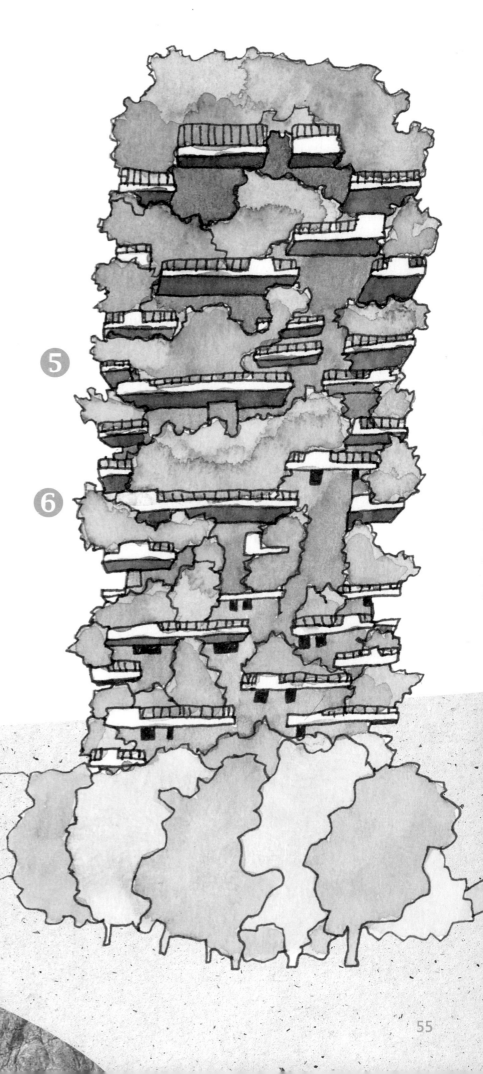

Space in the cities is becoming in-creasingly scarce, and the air quality is often poor. So the Malaysian architects Hamzah and Yeang hit upon the idea of building skyscraper-like *vertical parks*.

5 An architectural tree in the urban jungle: The Editt tower, just under construction in Singapore, is designed to have twenty-six stories. More than half of the façade will be planted with greenery.

An ingenious irrigation system will ensure that water is always avail-able in the tower, both for watering plants and for flushing toilets!

6 The tower's plants create a green microclimate*, which will improve Singapore's air quality. The building also has eco-friendly air conditioning and solar panels.

Architecture in fast forward

The First Architecture

Ancient Egypt

Ancient Greece

Ancient Rome

It took our ancestors a long time to "invent" architecture. Two million years ago, human-like beings were constantly on the move, sleeping in trees and caves. It wasn't until about 10,000 B.C. that people began to make oblong huts out of branches and leaves. At the same time, they developed the first true agriculture. Human communities could now truly settle down.

Over time, round straw huts and mud villages replaced the earlier structures.

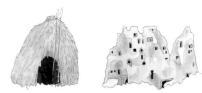

Then about 7,000 B.C., some clever ancestor invented mud-bricks; and around 4,000 B.C., the wheel was created. Finally it was possible to build cities, and Jericho is considered one of the earliest.

Egyptian architects were able to calculate astonishingly well even without computers, and they came up with some truly complicated geometric buildings. Their triangular pyramids were burial chambers for Egyptian kings, or pharaohs. These giant stone creations were so well constructed that they can still be marveled at today, 4,500 years later.

The Great Pyramid at Giza is one of the Seven Wonders of the World, and it's the only one that is still standing. Pyramids look like simple buildings. The base of each structure is in the form of a square. Yet we still don't know exactly how the ancient Egyptians assembled these buildings' heavy stone blocks so perfectly and so high.

Sand, wind, and robbers have carried away the white marble casing stones that originally covered the pyramids. In addition, the pyramids' mummies—the embalmed corpses of the dead pharaohs—were frequently stolen.

The ancient Greeks built architecture at a frenzied pace throughout the entire Greek region. The most important of these buildings were temples, each one dedicated to a specific god. And the good old Greeks had a great number of gods to worship! Temple architecture featured columns* and their capitals*—or the upper ends of the columns.

Each period in ancient Greek history had its own favorite style of column. The earliest was the Doric (1). Then came the Ionic (2) and the Corinthian (3).

1 2 3

And the Greeks loved to decorate their temples with sculptures—especially on the frieze* (4) and the pediments* (5).

5 4

The Romans copied endlessly from the Greeks, using Greek styles for their columns and temples. But they also developed new and improved ways of building. Roman architects used concrete, mortar, and the semi-circular arch to create a remarkable variety of structures.

These included aqueducts for supplying water to cities, sports stadiums (including the Colosseum) for entertaining the public, and giant bathhouses (thermae) that served as important meeting places.

Ca. 390 000 – 4000 B.C.   3000–2000 B.C.   600–300 B.C.   Ca. 200 B.C.–300 A.D.

56

From huts to cathedrals

Byzantine

The Middle Ages

Romanesque

Gothic

Byzantine

In A.D. 330, the Roman Emperor Constantine founded a new city that would replace Rome as the capital of his empire. This city, which had been called Byzantium, was given a new name: Constantinople. Constantine was a great admirer of Christianity, and he wanted to build "houses" where all Christian believers could gather. The basilica*, a type of structure invented by the Romans, soon became the form that all Christian churches would take. Basilicas are composed of an empty nave with many columns, and some were surmounted by a large dome.

Hagia Sophia in Constantinople (now Istanbul) is the most famous domed basilica. The construction of its huge, freestanding dome was a colossal achievement. This dome was made possible by means of special vaults and a particular kind of mortar.

Hagia Sophia also has ornate decoration and fine alabaster windows—typical features of "Byzantine" architecture.

Ca. A.D. 300–1450

The Middle Ages

After the fall of the Roman Empire, Europe was in constant motion. Groups of people began to migrate to new areas, but this movement often resulted in warlike confrontations. The migrating people needed safe places to live. So they sought out areas where they could see their enemies easily (such as hilltops) or places that offered them protection (such as islands or even old Roman fortifications). They also began building their own defensive structures, complete with walls and ditches. These structures would eventually develop into full-fledged castles.

Castles often had towers or a keep from which their inhabitants could keep a close eye on the surrounding area. Cisterns and wells were indispensible for providing water. After the Middle Ages, many castles were turned into palaces.

Ca. A.D. 450–1500

Romanesque

As the Middle Ages progressed Christianity grew increasingly powerful in Europe. Emperors and kings were now seen as being under God's special protection.

Around A.D. 1000, churches experienced a real construction boom, and architects departed more and more from ancient Roman models. They developed a new style that is now called the Romanesque.

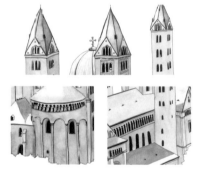

This style would use traditional Roman arches and massive vaults, but it would also include "cutting-edge" features such as dwarf galleries*, portals (grand doorways) filled with sculptures, and richly carved capitals*.

Ca. 1000–1200

Gothic

Whenever something really new takes place, various conditions have to come together. During the middle ages, kings were constantly at war with one another, merchants and other groups were becoming more important in society, and cities were beginning to grow. All of this turbulence made Europeans long even more for God—a single power who was above all worldly things.

In order to be closer to God, architects developed a new type of church: the Gothic cathedral. With their pointed arches and thin walls, these buildings rose upwards towards heaven—carrying their vaults to dizzying heights. Vast colored windows bathed the cathedrals in "divine" light. In England, new forms of this style continued to be built even into the twentieth century.

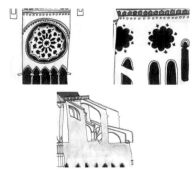

Ca. 1200–1500

Architecture in fast forward

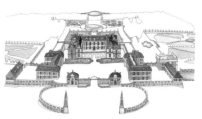

Renaissance

Baroque

Classicism

Historicism/ Gothic Revival

The origins of the Renaissance (or "rebirth") were in Italy. Italian merchants became interested in art and the culture of ancient Rome. Famous scholars from throughout the world came to Italy to study and teach. And the rediscovery of one Roman work, Vitruvius' *Ten Books on Architecture* from the first century A.D., triggered a building boom in the antique style. Renaissance architects used ancient principles of symmetry* to create harmonious proportions. Roman-style columns, pediments*, and arches also made the buildings' façades look elegant. Unlike the vast Gothic cathedrals, Renaissance architecture was designed to be "human-sized", reflecting the importance of individual people in Renaissance thought.

The "human-sized" Renaissance style was followed by a very different countermovement called the Baroque—a style famous for its love of splendor. European kings now believed themselves to be the center of the world, and they had magnificent palaces constructed, including Versailles. The Catholic Church erected lavishly decorated houses of worship. Musicians such as Bach and Handel composed glorious music, and painters such as Rubens created monumental artworks with oversized, voluptuous human characters.

Ornate stucco (colored plaster) decoration, *rocaille* (decoration in the form of a shell), *putti* (little angels), and scrollwork (entwined decoration of stucco or wood) were used to create triumphant façades. Barrel vaults and curved walls made baroque buildings appear even larger than they actually were.

The French Revolution in 1789 shook up not only society but architecture as well. The power of traditional kings and queens was being questioned, and no one wanted baroque sumptuousness any longer. Architects once again looked to classical antiquity for inspiration.

So-called "classicist" buildings soon transformed cities in Europe and elsewhere. Museums, theaters, government buildings, and even churches were made to look like ancient temples, with symmetrical* façades and Greek- or Roman-style columns*, capitals*, entablatures*, friezes*, and pediments*.

And since people were already busy reviving earlier building styles, in the mid- and late nineteenth century both the Gothic and the Renaissance also experienced revivals. This movement was called Historicism, and it affected both public and private buildings. Historicist architecture was built for the church and state. It was also commissioned by factory owners and other newly wealthy people—people who wanted mansions, villas, and other "monuments" built for themselves.

Some of these monumental homes looked like castles out of the Middle Ages, while others looked like Renaissance townhouses or baroque palaces. Their appearance was in stark contrast to many of the plain-looking factory buildings and other industrial structures.

Historicist architecture was popular for a long time in England, especially during the sixty-four-year reign of Queen Victoria. In fact, these buildings are often known as "Victorian" in style.

Ca. 1400–1600

Ca. 1600–1770

Ca. 1770–1850

Ca. 1830–1900

From decorative to practical

Industrialization

During the eighteenth century in England, factories started to produce iron in abundance. Architects soon began using this hard iron to construct bridges, glass palaces, greenhouses, train stations, and factories.

Such creations were both durable and practical, perfect for the hard-working era of industrialization. And some of them also had a delicate beauty—using rivets, buttresses, arches, and glass to create walls and roofs that resembled lace-like filigree*.

All of these new building types required architects to have a thorough knowledge of industrial materials. Thus many builders acquired a new name: engineer.

Art Nouveau/ Jugendstil

In many large cities such as Paris, Budapest, Vienna, and Barcelona, the industrial style developed further. Objects and buildings of daily use—including vases, tiles, lamps, outhouses, and subway stations—were produced in large numbers using industrial techniques. Yet they were still supposed to look individual and "natural". So their designers and architects began to imitate natural forms with "hard" materials such as glass and iron. This new style, often called *Art Nouveau or Jugendstil,* featured flowers and leaves in irregular and ornate forms.

The most dramatic Art Nouveau building, designed by Spanish architect Antoni Gaudí, was the church of Sagrada Família in Barcelona. Gaudí wanted everything in the church to appear as if it grew there by chance. The Sagrada Família's design is so complicated that it is still under construction today.

Art Déco

In the 1920s, the flowery Art Nouveau was replaced by a new style with dynamic forms, precious materials, and intense colors. This style was called Art Déco, and it became highly fashionable. Competitions arose among the builders of skyscrapers in New York City, and soon dozens of elegant Art Déco buildings rose toward the clouds.

These structures were made to look eye-catching and extravagant, partly through the use of shiny chrome, special lighting, flat surfaces, and symmetrical sunburst patterns. Even the insides of the buildings were fancy, with luxurious rooms, staircases, and office furnishings.

Art Déco style came to symbolize the 1920s and 30s, not only in skyscrapers like the Empire State Building and the Chrysler Tower but also in the swanky sets of Hollywood movies!

Bauhaus

Practical and beautiful, artistic but not too fancy, enduring and timeless: This is how architects, artists, and craftsmen pictured a new style for a new age. Everything should fit together: The dishes should fit the kitchen, the room should fit the building, and the individual should fit the room.

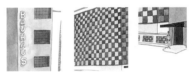

Many of the new artists came to study and work at the Bauhaus—a famous German art school in Weimar and Dessau. They wanted to do away with the ornate decoration of the past, and they designed buildings and objects using only basic shapes. These designs were meant to make the function of the building or object visible. Simplicity had become chic.

Bauhaus artists designed apartment buildings, chairs, tables, lamps, and even toothpicks with great care and attention.

Ca. 1780–1900   Ca. 1880–1920   Ca. 1920–1940   Ca. 1920–1960

Architecture in fast forward

1940 ▶▶ 1960 ▶▶ 1970 ▶▶ 1980 ▶▶ 2000

Brutalism

"Beton brut" is French for "exposed concrete", or walls in which the rough concrete material can still be seen. During the mid-1900s, this way of building gave rise to a style known as Brutalism. Brutalist architecture is known for its stark geometric shapes, which seem to fit together like toy blocks.

These buildings are rarely charming or quaint, often looking like raw rocks or caves. Their appearance—austere, broken up, and almost ugly—may reflect the suffering that Europeans experienced during World War II. Swiss-French architect Le Corbusier helped introduce the style. Corbusier's chapel in Ronchamp, France was one of the earliest buildings to use beton brut extensively. But the chapel's graceful curves look very different from most Brutalist architecture.

Spaceship Architecture

When the first man set foot on the Moon in 1969, space travel and science were all the rage—and shows about space were among the most popular on television. Architects too began to design buildings that used the new scientific tools of the space age.

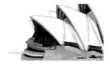

Houses were built with metal, Plexiglass, and new kinds of plastics. These materials could be used to make unusual forms and shapes. So builders were able to create houses that looked like vehicles or strange objects from the future. The Opera House in Sydney, Australia was designed to resemble a futuristic* sailboat gliding through the water.

Rainbow Architecture

Friedensreich Hundertwasser hated right angles. This Austrian architect had travelled widely, and he had soaked up the building styles of other countries. But he also admired the forms, shapes, and colors found in nature. Hundertwasser came to believe that nature should become part of architecture—and that buildings should help bring people closer to nature.

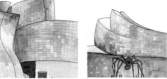

So Friedensreich began designing buildings that looked like no one else's. He used labyrinths, snail-like shapes, and snake-like forms—ideas that came from the natural world. He even brought nature directly into his buildings, putting trees and watercourses on his roofs and walls. Hundertwasser's buildings are also famous for the rainbow of colors they display—brightening up the gray cities in which they stand.

Modern Landmarks

New architecture can come in all kinds of crazy shapes. Some buildings look like a giant has stepped on them, while others resemble toppled tin cans! Straight edges have become a thing of the past. And the sparkly, shiny new building materials—which include all kinds of metals and plastics—make these structures stand out even more.

The boldest new buildings are designed to be exciting and fun. They are meant to stand out in the places where they are located—to be true landmarks. In northern Spain, one such landmark is the Guggenheim Museum Bilbao. Its architect, Frank Gehry, used sophisticated computer programs to make his architectural dream into a reality.

Ca. 1950–1970   Ca. 1960–1980   Ca. 1970–2000   Ca. 1990–the present

From concrete to plant towers

Dynamic Architecture

Blobitecture

Buildings of the Future

The ancient Romans may have been the first people to entertain huge crowds in gigantic stadiums. Roman amphitheaters like the Colosseum brought thrilling sports and other events to the masses. Even today, the Colosseum is a grand architectural icon*.

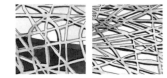

Today when cities host massive sporting events, like the Olympic Games, they often create buildings that are just as innovative as the Colosseum was in its own day. In 1972, for example, the futuristic* roof of the Olympic stadium in Munich, Germany became world famous. Then in 2008, the world turned its gaze towards another great Olympic building: the Bird's Nest stadium in Beijing, China. This building may look like a fragile bird's nest, but in truth it is incredibly strong and stable. Its architects used ideas from nature and from cutting-edge computer programs to produce a structure both delicate and powerful.

In the 1990s, yet another computer program created a new trend in architecture. This amazing achievement was called CAD, or computer-aided design, and today no architect can imagine doing without it. CAD made it possible to design buildings that resemble eggplants, creatures from the deep sea, or blob-like beings from outer space! The shapes of these buildings helped name the new trend—blobitecture.

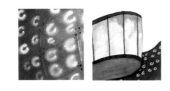

With the help of CAD, structures can now be filled with glass and shiny plastic. When these buildings first appeared, people were flabbergasted at their appearance. They looked like giant alien creatures in the middle of the city. One Blob building has stood in London since 2002: the City Hall. This structure, which houses London's mayor, is not only remarkable to look at—it is also energy efficient!

Architects today are concerned about problems that may affect our society and our world—climate change, the ozone hole, air pollution, and the loss of natural resources*. How can modern houses be built in harmony with nature? In many parts of the world, buildings need to withstand earthquakes and storms. Other buildings should have "green walls" that generate microclimates* and help protect their inhabitants from environmental pollution. Still others may need to exist on water in case coastal areas become flooded because of climate change.

To achieve all of these goals, many architects have been studying buildings from the earliest days of architecture. Certain features of cave dwellings, treehouses, and other early structures are being used to design buildings of the future.

Glossary

Amazons: Female warriors who appeared in many ancient Greek stories, including *The Iliad*, a famous tale by the poet Homer.

Amphitheater: A large, oval-shaped Roman building designed to house fights and other forms of entertainment for large crowds. The term amphitheater comes from Greek words meaning "theater in the round".

Architectural icons: Buildings or structures that everyone recognizes immediately, such as the Eiffel Tower, the Statue of Liberty, or the Colosseum.

Base: The lowest part of a column or a building.

Basilica: A type of church with a high nave and two or four lower side aisles. This type of building developed from Roman basilicas, which were halls used to house markets or courts of law. The basilica remained the most important form of Christian church into the nineteenth century.

Byzantine: The building style in southeastern Europe for hundreds of years, which combined features of Roman architecture and Middle Eastern architecture. The most famous Byzantine church is Hagia Sophia, which was built in Constantinople (present-day Istanbul) in the A.D. 500s.

A **capital** is the uppermost part of a column. In the Romanesque period, capitals were often block-shaped with sides that rounded out towards the bottom. Many of them were richly carved with figures and plants.

Centaur: A legendary creature from ancient Greece that was half human and half horse. Centaurs were considered troublemakers.

Chase: To carve or cut metal into delicate patterns. People can also chase wood, stucco, and other materials.

Columns are vertical, pole-like forms that often help support a building. They usually consist of a base, shaft, and capital. Ancient Greek columns came in three basic types (or orders):
Doric—a stocky column without a base and with smooth bulging capitals;
Ionic—a slim column with a base and with capitals that have volutes (rounded, scroll-like forms) on the sides;
Corinthian—an even slimmer column with a capital formed out of large, sculpted leaves.

Compound pillar: A column that contains many smaller columns.

Cornice: A horizontal strip along a wall that often includes decoration called molding. Cornices jut outwards from the wall and help make the outside of the building look beautiful.

Crenellation: A wall often built along the top of a castle. This type of wall has regular gaps in it, from which medieval soldiers could shoot arrows at an approaching enemy.

Dwarf gallery: A type of arcade (or series of arches) just beneath the roof of a church or other building. Dwarf galleries were often used as decoration in Romanesque architecture.

Entablature: Structures that lie above the columns in temples and other buildings. Entablatures include the cornice and the frieze.

Extravagance: In architecture, extravagance means the use of striking or expensive materials or decoration—such as the fancy steel pyramid atop the Chrysler Building in New York City.

Façade: A particular side of a building, usually the front side.

Filigree: An elegant word for something that appears very fine and delicate.

Frieze: A narrow horizontal band around the top of a building. Friezes usually include carved decoration.

Functional: In architecture, this term refers to a building that is designed to be completely practical. Most functionalist buildings, such as factories, do not have much decoration.

Futuristic: A term used to describe something looks like it's far ahead of its time (from the Latin word *futurus*).

Groin vault: A type of vault (or part of a ceiling) that consists of two semi-circular "barrel" vaults that intersect at right angles. Groin vaults resemble rounded, cross-like shapes, and they became popular in medieval church architecture.

Hinduism: The world's third largest religion, after Christianity and Islam. Hinduism arose in India as early as 2000 B.C.

Humanism: A philosophy that began during the Renaissance and was inspired by the writings of ancient Greek scholars. A central idea in Humanism is the dignity and uniqueness of the human being.

Industrialization: The period of history in which factories, trains, and other forms of modern industry first developed. New ways of producing iron made industrialization possible, and architects began to design industrial buildings with this material. Such builders soon became known as engineers.

Irrational: Something that does not seem logical. In architecture, this term refers to parts of a building that do not have a clear purpose.

A **lackey** was formerly a servant in uniform.

Materials science is the study of the properties of metals and other materials.

Mausoleum: A building designed as a tomb. Many mausoleums look like small palaces, and they were often constructed for famous, wealthy, or powerful individuals.

Microclimate: A small area in which a specific climate is created by the plants growing there. In buildings, microclimates can exist within courtyards, greenhouses, or other enclosed spaces.

A **minaret** is the thin, often decorated tower of a mosque, from which the call to prayers is made. Mosques can have up to eight minarets.

Mughal style: The style of architecture in India when it was ruled by the Mughal Empire, primarily during the sixteenth and seventeenth centuries. Mughal emperors had their architects design magnificent structures that mixed Arabic, Persian, and Indian traditions. These buildings often had large domes, colorful decoration, and keyhole-shaped windows. The most famous example of Mughal architecture is the Taj Mahal.

A **mosque** is the name for a Muslim house of worship.

Mummy: A dead body that has been preserved by brushing it with liquid chemicals and wrapping it in cloths. Many ancient Egyptian mummies are still in pristine condition today.

Muslim is a follower of Islam, the religion introduced to the world by the prophet Mohammed around A.D. 620, in what is now Saudi Arabia.

Olympic gods: The family of ancient Greek gods that lived on Olympus, a mountain in Greece.

Ostentation: The display of great wealth and power.

Pediment is a triangular-shaped wall that often appears above the columns of classical temples. Pediments are usually decorated with sculptures.

Pilasters: Flat columns that are built into the wall. Pilasters usually do not support the structure. Instead, they play an important part of a building's design.

Plumb-bob, or plummet, is an instrument used to determine the exact vertical lines of a building.

A **prestige building** has to be striking and flaunt what it contains.

Postmodernism: A style that means "after Modernism", which had its heyday in the 1970s. Postmodern architects turned away from the "classical" Modernism of the Bauhaus—a style that featured angular shapes and little decoration. Instead, these designers often used curving shapes, bright colors, and decoration that reminded people of older architecture. Many postmodernist buildings were intended to be playful or humorous.

Recycling is when used or broken things are reprocessed and reused.

Relief: A carving in wood or stone that looks like it is raised up out of the surface. "High relief" is carved deeply into the wood or stone, making the carvings seem extremely three-dimensional. In "Bas (low) relief", the sculptor does not carve very deeply, and his designs appear rather flat.

Retro actually means "backwards", but it also refers to things that seem charming because of their age or things that are made to look as if they were old.

A **rotunda** is a structure built on a circular plan and generally surmounted by a dome.

Single-point perspective: A method used to make two-dimensional pictures look three-dimensional. In single-point perspective, all the lines of the picture converge toward a single "vanishing" point. This technique was made popular during the Renaissance.

Statics: Calculations that are made to prevent a building from falling down. All architecture needs to be at "static equilibrium", meaning that all parts of the building should be constructed so that they remain stable.

Stucco: Plaster decorations on the walls and ceilings. Stucco decoration often looks very fancy and opulent.

Symmetry: In a symmetrical structure, the right side of the building is the mirror image of the left side of a building—and vice versa. Symmetry helps make buildings look harmonious, and it is used in many styles of architecture.

Troubadour: A type of entertainer who was popular during the Middle Ages. Troubadours often travelled from castle to castle, entertaining the lords and ladies by singing songs and reciting poems.

Utopians are people who develop ideas that are intended to make society better. Often these ideas are not (yet) possible to achieve in reality.

Visionaries are people who can predict things that will happen in the future. Visionary artists often incorporate such predictions into their work

World expositions or **world's fairs:** Large fairs that take place every few years at different places around the world. These events began in nineteenth century as a way of showing people the most important new inventions in engineering, science, architecture, and other fields. Some of the buildings constructed for world's fairs have become famous, such as the Eiffel Tower in Paris.

Abbreviations
BC: Before Christ
AD: After the birth of Christ (from the latin *Anno Domini*, or "the year of our Lord")

© Prestel Verlag, Munich · London · New York, 2012. 2nd printing 2013

Library of Congress Control Number is available; British Library Cataloguing-in-Publication Data: a catalogue record for this book is available from the British Library; Deutsche Nationalbibliothek holds a record of this publication in the Deutsche Nationalbibliografie; detailed bibliographical data can be found under: http://dnb.ddb.de

Prestel,
a member of Verlagsgruppe Random House GmbH

www.prestel.com

Translation: Cynthia Hall
Editorial direction: Doris Kutschbach
Project management: Sabine Tauber
Copyeditor: Brad Finger
Design, layout and typesetting: Christine Paxmann, text • konzept • grafik
Production: Astrid Wedemeyer
Art Direction: Cilly Klotz
Origination: Reproline mediateam, München
Printing and Binding: TBB, a.s.

Verlagsgruppe Random House FSC® N001967
The FSC®-certified paper Hello Fat Matt produced
by mill Condat has been supplied by Deutsche Papier.

ISBN 978-3-7913-7113-9